# " Poor Marta "

## Author and Illustrator
## Claire Boggs

Marta was born in Guatemala. She was very poor. Her mother loved her very much, but she sent Marta to live with a neighbor, because Marta's mother had so many children and not enough food to feed them.

Marta was four years old when she went to live with the neighbor. She had to wash clothes. She had to wash dishes. She had to make tortillas. She did not have time to play.

Sometimes Marta was hungry in her new house, too. One day she climbed up into a tree to get an apple. She heard footsteps coming. It was the mean man of her new family. She was afraid of him. She sat very still. She was glad that he did not look up into the tree.

When he passed by, Marta hurried to her room. She hid in the closet to eat the apple. It tasted so good.

As Marta grew up the mean family did not buy her any new clothes. Marta had a little green apron she wore when she worked. She worked very hard washing clothes in the big blue sink.

The lady would send Marta to the store. Marta liked to go to the store. Sometimes she would play on her way. But if she were late, the mean man would hit her very hard.

Poor Marta. She was very sad.

The neighbors saw that Marta was sad. They wanted to help her, but they could only pray for Marta.

One day when Marta was six years old, she was sent to the store. "Bring me two eggs and a book of matches," yelled the mean lady. "And don't come back until you have the right ones," she said.

Marta ran to the closest store. The lady at the store said in Spanish, "¡No hay!*" So Marta ran to the next store. "¡No hay!" Then she ran to another store. "¡No hay!"

* In Spanish "No hay" means "There is none."
"Hay" is pronounced "eye."

# Tienda Maria

It was getting late. Marta was afraid to go home without the eggs and matches. She crossed the big highway. She was careful to look both ways for cars. Finally, a person in the store said, "¡Sí* hay!"

*In Spanish "Sí" means "yes."*

Marta was happy! Then she looked up and saw that it was dark! "Oh, no," she thought. "They are going to hit me!" She was really scared.

"I just can't go back there," she decided. Marta was so afraid. Then she saw someone waiting for her in the doorway. She ran up to the door, threw the eggs and matches into the house, and ran away as fast as her little legs could carry her.

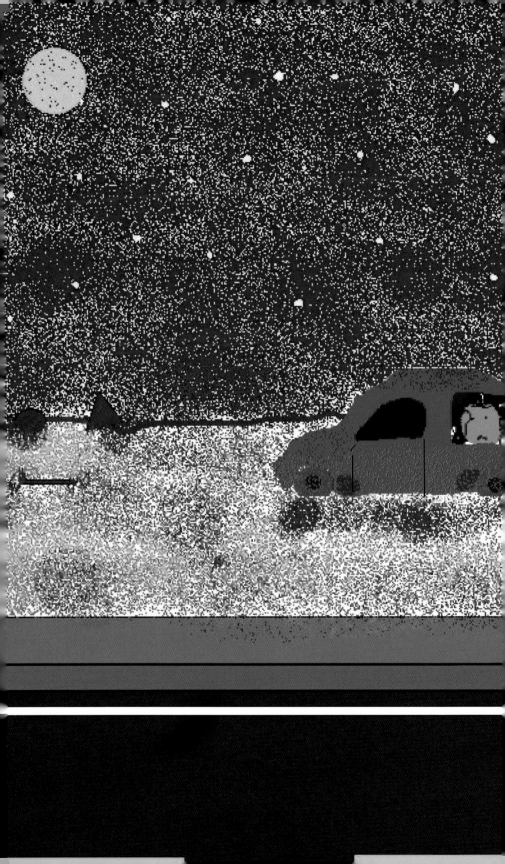

Nearby there was an old abandoned car where she once had played. "That is where I can hide," she thought.
It was dark and cold and lonely.
Marta was so scared. Poor Marta!

That night Marta's neighbors were coming home from church. They walked near the old car. They saw Marta curled up in the car. "Marta," said the neighbor, "What are you doing outside so late? Your family will be looking for you!"

Marta started to cry. She told her story to the nice lady. The lady prayed for Marta. The neighbors were afraid to take Marta to the mean people's house. They decided to take her to the Children's Home instead.

That night, the mean family went looking for Marta. They went to Marta's old house. "Where is she?" They screamed. "We will have you put in jail!" They yelled outside the door. "Marta belongs to us," they said. But Marta was safe in the Children's Home.

Marta's mother knew of a missionary family who would help her. She asked if the missionaries could find a good Christian family for Marta. "We do not have enough food or clothes for Marta in our house," said Marta's birth mother.

Marta met Mama Clarita at the Children's Home. Marta had never met a missionary before. Right away she felt a special love from Mama Clarita. Marta was no longer afraid. "Marta," said Mama Clarita, "We know a family who would like to adopt a little girl."

**A** letter had come to the missionaries saying:

Dear Missionary,

We have one little boy and we are praying that God will give us a little girl. Please write and let us know if you have a little girl who needs a good Christian home. We want to find just the child God has for us.

Thank you,
Mr. and Mrs. Moon

This wonderful family adopted Marta as their own little girl. Mama Clarita went with Marta in the airplane to meet her new family.

Marta's new family loves Jesus very much. They took Marta to church. She made many friends who helped her learn English.

Marta listened to stories about Jesus. She heard that if she would accept Jesus into her life, she would live with Him forever in Heaven.

Marta prayed and invited Jesus into her heart. Now Marta has her new name written down in <u>The Book of Life</u> in Heaven.

Marta is happy with her new family and her new name:
                    Marta Lidia Moon

## To Parents:

*The Bible tells us that Jesus saves.*

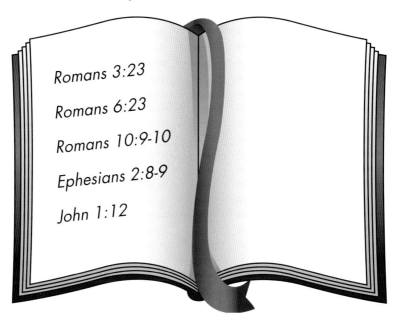

Romans 3:23

Romans 6:23

Romans 10:9-10

Ephesians 2:8-9

John 1:12

# "Poor Marta"

First Edition

Copyright © 2004 by **Mama Clarita Stories**

Library of Congress Control Number 2004108325

ISBN 0-9755283-0-0

Graphic Design & Book Layout by Larry G. Nichols II
Printed in the U.S.A. by Mennonite Press, Inc., Newton, Kansas